A New True Book

SATURN

By Dennis B. Fradin

CHILDRENS PRESS®

CHICAGO

Voyager photograph of one of Saturn's moons

For Danny Newman

PHOTO CREDITS
John Forsberg—8, 9
Lee Meents—26 (bottom)
The Bettmann Archive—10, 13 (both), 17, 19 (both), 22 (right), 25
NASA—Cover, 2, 4 (top), 6, 15 (left), 20, 21 (both), 22 (left), 24, 26 (top), 30, 33, 34 (both), 39, 43
NASA-JET PROPULSION LAB—18, 37 (both), 40, 41, 42, 45
National Optical Astronomy Observatories—4 (bottom)
James Oberg—29
Yerkes Observatory Photograph—15 (right), 28

Library of Congress Cataloging-in-Publication Data

Fradin, Dennis B.
    Saturn / by Dennis B. Fradin.
        p.   cm. — (A New true book)
    Includes index.
    Summary: Discusses the characteristics of Saturn and how information about it has been gathered from ancient times to the present day when the Voyager probes sent back a series of photographs of the ringed planet.
    ISBN 0-516-01166-9
    1. Saturn (Planet)—Juvenile literature. [1. Saturn (Planet). 2. Planets.] I. Title.
QB671.F73   1989   88-39117
512.4'6—dc19   CIP
                                          AC

TABLE OF CONTENTS

The Lagoon Nebula in Sagittarius (above). The solar
telescope at Kitt Peak Observatory near Tucson, Arizona (below).

THE SOLAR SYSTEM

Stars are giant balls of hot, glowing gas. There are many millions of stars in space. We can see about 2,000 of them on a clear night. A telescope reveals millions more.

All the stars except one can be seen only at night. The one that shows up in the daytime is the Sun. In fact, the Sun causes the daytime. Compared to

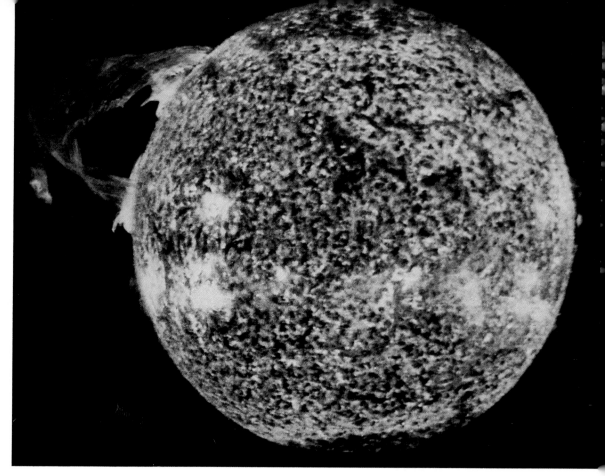

Skylab photographed the Sun, the star closest to Earth.

other stars, the Sun is just average in brightness, hotness, and size. Why, then, does it look so bright? Why does it feel so warm on our skin?

Why does it look so much bigger than other stars? The answer is that the Sun is much closer to us than the other stars.

Planets are big objects that orbit a star. It is thought that many stars besides the Sun have planets. The Sun has nine known planets.

Mercury is the planet closest to the Sun. Venus comes second. Our home

Sun

Mercury

Venus

Earth

Mars

Jupiter

planet—the Earth—comes
third. Then come Mars,
Jupiter, Saturn, Uranus,
Neptune, and Pluto.

Seven of the nine
planets have moons that
orbit them. Earth has one
moon. Mars has two
moons, and Jupiter has 16.
Saturn is the moon

champion. It has at least 19 moons.

The Sun and all objects that orbit it are called the *Solar System.* The Sun is the biggest object in the Solar System. The planets and their moons are the Solar System's other main objects.

Woodcut showing Arab astronomers studying the stars.

ANCIENT PEOPLE
SAW SATURN

There is a way to tell
planets from stars with just
our eyes. Stars twinkle.
Planets shine steadily. The
reason is that stars shine
by their own light. Planets

10

have no light of their own.
Instead, they reflect the
steady light of the Sun.

Thousands of years ago,
people saw five planets.
They were Mercury, Venus,
Mars, Jupiter, and Saturn.
The ancient people did not
know that the Earth is a
planet, too. The last three
planets—Uranus, Neptune,
and Pluto—were not found
until after the telescope
was invented.

Saturn was known by various names to the ancient people. The Egyptians were thought to have called the planet "Horus." But the ancient Romans provided most of the names we use for the planets. For example, one planet looked blood-red. Blood reminded the Romans of war. They named the red planet Mars, after their god of war.

The Egyptian hawk-god
Horus (above) and Saturn, the
Roman god of farming (right)

The Romans had an
important god of farming
named Saturn. They gave
his name to the yellow-
white planet that today we
call Saturn.

SATURN THROUGH EARLY TELESCOPES

Until the 1600s, nothing was known about conditions on the planets. Our eyes alone cannot see details on the planets.

About the year 1608 telescopes were invented. These instruments make distant objects look closer. The first astronomer to use a telescope was Galileo (1564-1642) of Italy.

The Milky Way Galaxy (left) and Galileo (right)

Galileo viewed many
objects in the heavens. He
discovered that the Moon
has mountains. He learned
that the Milky Way is
made of stars. He also
saw something strange
about Saturn.

Saturn seemed to have a handle on each side. Galileo did not know what the handles were. He thought they might be moons. But if they were moons, why did they seem to stay for a long time in the same place?

Galileo's telescope was too small to reveal the truth. The handles were really rings around Saturn. Soon after Galileo died, more powerful telescopes

Christian Huygens

were built. Some of the best were made by Christian Huygens (1629-1695) of The Netherlands.

Today, many people gasp when they first see Saturn's rings through a

Color photograph of Saturn

telescope. Saturn is one of
the loveliest objects in the
heavens. Perhaps Huygens
gasped when he aimed his
telescope at Saturn and
became the first person
to see that it has rings!

BIGGER TELESCOPES
SHOW MORE OF SATURN

Bigger and better telescopes were built later. Astronomers made many discoveries with them. Some had to do with Saturn.

The Mayall Telescope (left) at Kitt Peak Observatory in the United States and the Schmidt Telescope (right) at Siding Spring Observatory in Australia

Some of the moons of Saturn: Dione (front), Tethys and Mimas (right), Enceladus and Rhea (left), Titan (top right)

Many moons were found to orbit Saturn. Saturn's biggest moon first was seen by Christian Huygens in 1655. It was named Titan. Between

1671 and 1684 four more of Saturn's moons were found by an astronomer named Cassini. Two more were discovered by William Herschel in 1789. Two more were discovered in the 1800s. By the year 1898 astronomers knew Saturn had nine moons.

Enceladus (left) and Hyperion (right)

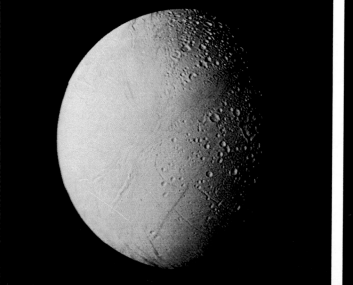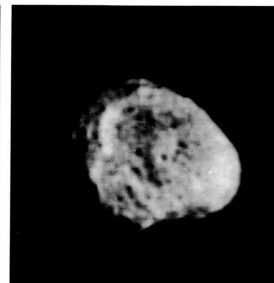

James Clark Maxwell (right) and a color photograph of Saturn's rings

More was learned about Saturn's ring system, too. At first it had been thought Saturn had one ring. Larger, more powerful, telescopes showed Saturn had several rings.

Many people had
thought Saturn's rings were
solid. In 1857 James Clark
Maxwell proved
mathematically that the
rings could not be solid.
Scientists believe the rings
are made of billions of
particles. These particles
are always orbiting Saturn.

Telescopes also revealed
that we do not see a solid
surface when we view
Saturn. We see clouds. By

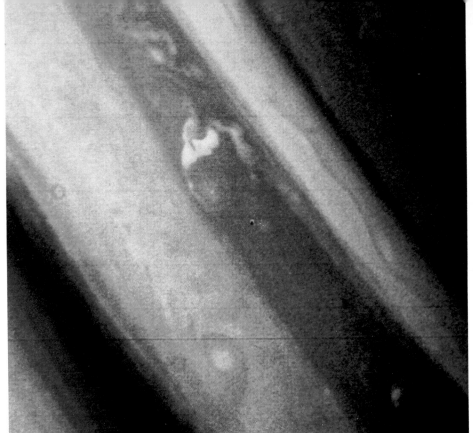

Color
photograph
of Saturn's
clouds

watching spots on its
clouds, astronomers of the
1800s learned how long it
takes Saturn to spin once.
The ringed planet spins
once about every 10½
hours. This means that a

day on Saturn would be about 10½ hours long.

During the 1800s, astronomers also found a way to tell what heavenly bodies are made of. Tools called *spectroscopes* helped them. By the 1930s

Spectroscope used in 1887 could analyze both candle and gas light.

MERCURY

VENUS

EARTH

MARS

Voyager photograph of Saturn

JUPITER

SATURN

URANUS

NEPTUNE

PLUTO

it was known that Saturn's clouds contain substances that would poison people.

A few other basic facts also were known by then. Astronomers had long known that Saturn takes about 29½ years to go around the Sun. This means that a year on Saturn is about 29½ Earth-years long. It was known that Saturn is the second-biggest planet (after Jupiter). About 800 Earths could fit inside Saturn!

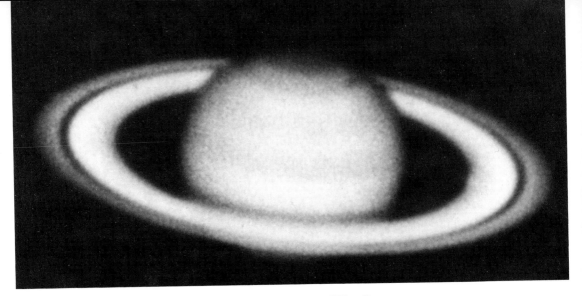

This 1911 photograph of Saturn shows you how difficult
it was for scientists to study this planet.

And it was known that
Saturn is much colder than
the Earth's North Pole.

But there still were
many questions about
Saturn, its rings, and its
moons. Not even our
biggest telescopes were
helping to answer those
questions.

FIRST SPACE PROBE TO SATURN !

The space age began in 1957, when Russia launched *Sputnik I.* This was the first artificial satellite to orbit the Earth.

Sputnik launched the world into the Space Age.

Astronauts explored the surface of the moon.

In 1969 the United States sent the first people to another heavenly body when it landed astronauts on the Moon.

The Moon is only about 240,000 miles away. That

is almost next door
compared to the planets.
The closest planets to
Earth—Venus and Mars—
are more than one
hundred times farther than
the Moon. People are not
likely to visit Mars until
well after the year 2000.
Visits to distant planets
like Saturn will not occur
until many years after that.

The United States and
Russia found a way to
explore the planets without

sending people. They sent *space probes*. These unmanned spacecraft sent pictures and data back to the Earth.

The United States launched the *Pioneer-Saturn* probe on April 6, 1973. It had two targets. First it was to fly near Jupiter. Then it was to become the first probe to fly near Saturn.

For over 1½ years *Pioneer-Saturn* traveled through space. In

Painting shows *Pioneer-Saturn* approaching Saturn.
Pioneer took the first closeup pictures of Saturn.

December 1974 it came
within about 25,000 miles
of Jupiter. It sent back
very good close-up
pictures of Jupiter. Then it
continued toward Saturn.

Pioneer photograph (above) and *Voyager* photograph (below) of Saturn

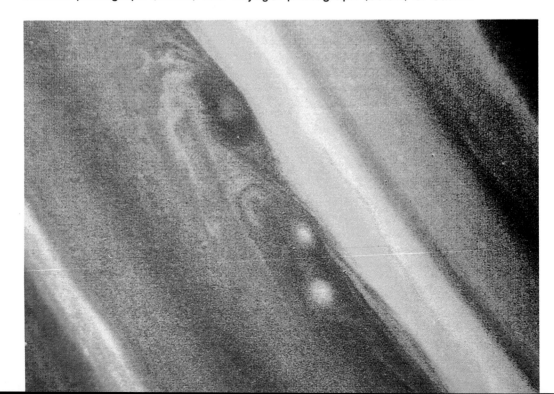

Pioneer-Saturn came to within 13,000 miles of Saturn in September 1979. The probe found that Saturn's clouds have swirls on them like Jupiter's clouds. These proved to be storms on Saturn. It found two new rings in Saturn's ring system. It also discovered that Saturn has a magnetic field hundreds of times stronger than the Earth's.

VOYAGER I AND II

Two other U.S. probes revealed even more about Saturn. They were *Voyager I* and *Voyager II. Voyager I* blasted off from Florida in August 1977. *Voyager II* blasted off from the same place that September. The *Voyagers* were to explore Jupiter first. Then they were to go on to Saturn, Uranus, and finally Neptune.

In 1979 the *Voyagers* sent back new information about Jupiter. For one thing, Jupiter was found to have a ring, much smaller than Saturn's rings. The *Voyagers* then were hurled toward Saturn.

Jupiter (left) and a close-up of its ring (right)

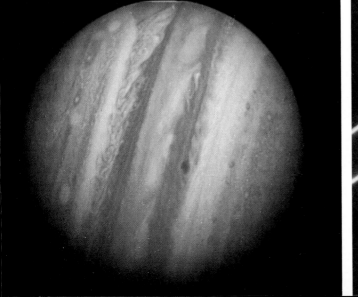

Voyager I reached within 80,000 miles of Saturn in November 1980. *Voyager II* came to within 65,000 miles of the ringed planet less than a year later. The *Voyagers* sent back more detailed pictures and a great deal of other information about Saturn and its moons.

It was learned that Saturn has more than just several rings. It has dozens and dozens of rings. The rings are made

Voyager photographed Saturn's rings from a distance of four million miles.

of dust and ice particles that range in size from specks to house-sized pieces.

Saturn also was found to have very strong winds. In places they blow at over 1,000 miles per hour. That

The *Voyager* spacecraft

is much stronger than the strongest hurricanes on the Earth!

The *Voyagers* taught us a great deal about Saturn's moons, too. Many of them are mainly ice. Titan— Saturn's largest moon—has

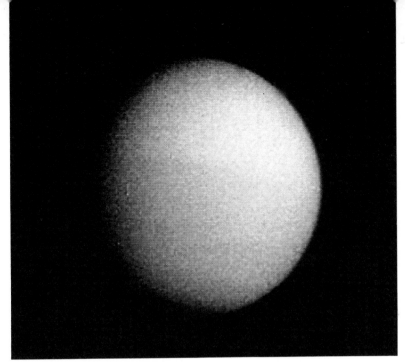

Titan

an atmosphere made up mostly of nitrogen. This means its atmosphere is somewhat like the Earth's. Several new moons were discovered, bringing Saturn's total to 19. More moons are yet to be discovered.

Different colors show scientists that Saturn's rings are made up of different substances.

LEARNING MORE ABOUT SATURN IN THE FUTURE

Scientists still have many questions about Saturn. How were its rings formed? Did they come from a moon that broke apart and began orbiting

Saturn? Were they leftover
bits from when Saturn was
formed? Or were they
created in another way?

Saturn is thought to be
mainly gas with a little
solid material deep inside
it. But no one has viewed
the planet's surface
beneath the clouds.

Saturn gives off a lot more heat than it gets from the Sun. This puzzles astronomers. Where does the heat come from? Why does Saturn have so many more moons than the Earth? And what is it like on the surfaces of those moons?

The answers won't just teach us more about Saturn. They may help us understand how the whole

Dione is one of Saturn's moons.

Solar System was formed. Future space probes alone may not provide all the answers. One day people may be sent to the lovely ringed planet to solve its mysteries.

FACTS ABOUT SATURN

Average Distance from Sun—
About 885 million miles

Closest Approach to Earth—
About 744 million miles

*Diameter—*About 74,600 miles

*Length of Day—*10 hours
and 39 minutes

*Length of Year—*About 29½
Earth-years

*Temperatures—*Nearly 300
degrees below zero F.

*Atmosphere—*Mainly
hydrogen and helium

*Number of Moons—*Over
20 (Saturn has the most
moons of any of the 9
planets)

*Weight of an Object on
Saturn That Would Weigh
100 Pounds on Earth—*116
pounds

*Average Speed as Saturn
Orbits the Sun—*About 6
miles per second

WORDS YOU SHOULD KNOW

ancient(AIN • shent)—very old

astronomers(ah • STRON • ih • merz)—people who study stars,
planets, and other heavenly bodies

atmosphere(AT • muss • feer)—the gases surrounding some
heavenly bodies

Earth(ERTH)—the planet (the 3rd from the Sun) on which we live

million(MILL • yun)—a thousand thousand (1,000,000)

moons(MOONZ)—natural objects that orbit most of the 9 planets;
Saturn is the moon champion with over 20

planets(PLAN • its)—large objects that orbit stars; the Sun has
9 planets

ringed planet(RINGD PLAN • it)—a nickname for Saturn

Saturn(SAT • ern) — the 6th planet from the Sun

Solar System(SO • ler SIS • tem) — the Sun and its "family" of objects

space probes(SPAISS PROHBZ) — unmanned spacecraft sent to study heavenly bodies

spectroscopes(SPEK • tra • skohpz) — instruments that help astronomers learn what heavenly bodies are made of

stars(STAHRZ) — giant balls of hot, glowing gas

Sun(SUN) — the yellow star that is the closest star to the Earth

telescopes(TEL • ih • skopes) — instruments that make distant objects look closer

INDEX

About the Author

Dennis Fradin attended Northwestern University on a partial creative scholarship and was graduated in 1967. His previous books include the Young People's Stories of Our States series for Childrens Press, and Bad Luck Tony for Prentice-Hall. In the True book series Dennis has written about astronomy, farming, comets, archaeology, movies, space colonies, the space lab, explorers, and pioneers. He is married and the father of three children.